Ancient Egyptian Civilization

Ancient Egyptian Hieroglyphs

by Kathy Allen

raintree
a Capstone company — publishers for children

Raintree is an imprint of Capstone Global Library Limited, a company incorporated in England and Wales having its registered office at 264 Banbury Road, Oxford, OX2 7DY – Registered company number: 6695582

www.raintree.co.uk
myorders@raintree.co.uk

Text © Capstone Global Library Limited 2016
The moral rights of the proprietor have been asserted.

Edited by Mari Bolte
Designed by Juliette Peters
Picture research by Marcie Spence
Production by Laura Manthe

ISBN 978 1 4747 1725 0
19 18 17 16 15
10 9 8 7 6 5 4 3 2 1

British Library Cataloguing in Publication Data
A full catalogue record for this book is available from the British Library.

Photo Credits
Art Resource, N.Y.: Alfredo Dagli Orti, 12, Werner Forman, 16; Bridgeman Art Library: British Museum, London, UK, 5, Egyptian National Museum, Cairo, Egypt, 14 (left), Look and Learn, 6, 25 (top), Louvre, Paris, France/Giraudon, 20, 25 (bottom), Royal Society, London, UK, 18; Corbis: Gianni Dagli Orti, 15, Sandro Vannini, 23, Thomas Hartwell, 17; Dreamstime: Jorge Farres Sanchez, 14 (right); Shutterstock: Bill McKelvie, 10, Dudarev Mikhail, design element, Efremova Irina, 21, Fedor Selivanov, cover, 8, Rafa Irusta, design element, Tawfik Deifalla, 24 (left), Vladimir Korostyshevskiy, 24 (right)

We would like to thank Jennifer Houser Wegner, PhD, for her invaluable help in the preparation of this book.

CONTENTS

Mysterious markings

In 1798, a group of French soldiers in Napoleon's army arrived in Egypt and were ordered to travel to Cairo on foot. It was a difficult trip at the hottest time of the year. The soldiers were not used to such heat or dry air. They were not prepared for a march through the desert. Many did not bring water. Dry biscuits were all they had to eat.

After many days in the sandy desert, the soldiers came upon an **oasis**. They saw a shimmering lake and palm trees. But as soon as they neared the water, it vanished. It was yet another **mirage**. When they began to see tombs and temples, they thought these, too, were tricks of the eye. When they touched the temples, they knew their visions were real. The structures were covered with some kind of picture writing. But nobody could read what it said.

oasis place in the desert where there is water

mirage something that appears to be there but is not

When a soldier found a giant stone near the town of Rosetta, he barely trusted his tired eyes. At first he saw more of the strange markings no one could read. But the Rosetta stone was different from the others. He recognized Greek text carved into the stone. Could this text help them decode the writing on the walls and sculptures around them? What would they learn from this lost language?

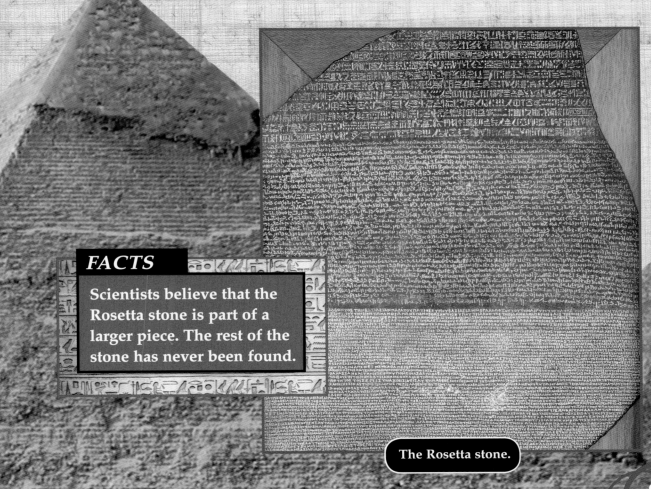

FACTS

Scientists believe that the Rosetta stone is part of a larger piece. The rest of the stone has never been found.

The Rosetta stone.

Chapter 1

Words of the gods

The soldiers did not know that the strange lettering was part of an ancient language. The markings were a type of writing called hieroglyphs. Hieroglyphic writing uses pictures to represent words. The word *hieroglyphs* means "God's words". Ancient Egyptians used these signs to tell tales of wars and gods. They carved them on tombs and temples. For more than 3,000 years, hieroglyphs were used to write their spoken language. But that skill was lost over time.

Scholars were brought to Egypt to study the stone.

It is easy to understand why hieroglyphs were difficult to read. They are much more than just rows of pictures. Hieroglyphs include signs that were pronounced and signs that weren't. Many signs can represent either an object or a sound. And some signs stand for both.

Signs that were pronounced are called phonograms. Some phonograms represented ideas. These signs are called ideograms. Each ideogram represented a word.

Ideograms

sound	symbol	meaning
r		"mouth"
pr		"house"
s		"man"
r^c		"sun"

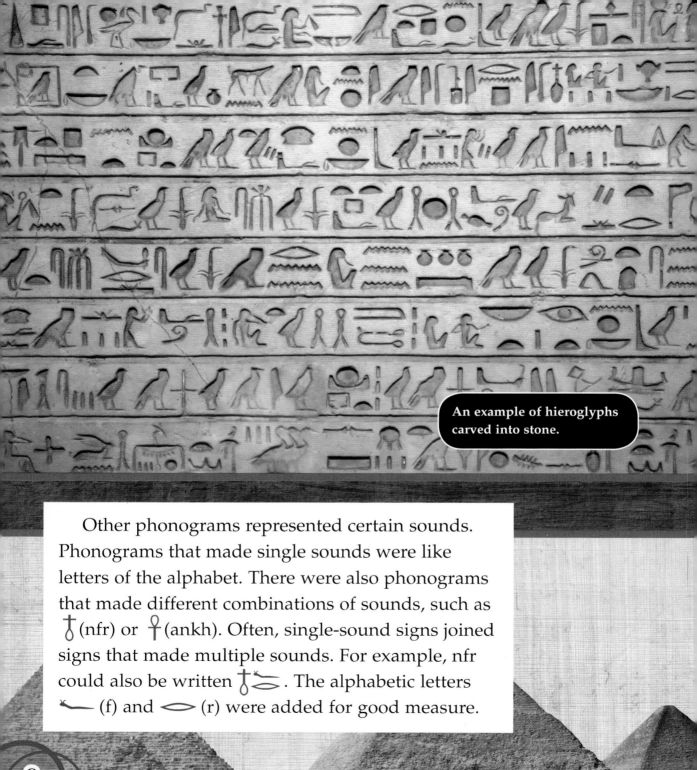

An example of hieroglyphs carved into stone.

Other phonograms represented certain sounds. Phonograms that made single sounds were like letters of the alphabet. There were also phonograms that made different combinations of sounds, such as ⌇(nfr) or ⌇(ankh). Often, single-sound signs joined signs that made multiple sounds. For example, nfr could also be written ⌇. The alphabetic letters ⌇ (f) and ⌇ (r) were added for good measure.

8

Signs that were not pronounced were called determinatives. These signs came at the end of the written word. They made the meaning of the word clearer to the reader.

Determinative

sound	symbol	meaning
dgỉ		"look"
šp		"blind"
dpt		"ship"
ḥdỉ		"sail downstream"

Sometimes ideograms were used as determinatives. They were not pronounced.

sound	symbol	meaning
hrw		"day"
wbn		"rise"
smr		"courtier"
ct		"room, chamber"
ȝḥ		"horizon"
ỉwnn		"sanctuary"

Temple of Rameses III in Luxor.

Hieroglyphs are usually read from right to left. But some monuments in Egypt have carvings that are read from left to right. This difference is because the hieroglyphs were also used to decorate objects. The words meant the same thing. They may have looked more balanced when written left to right.

It was important to the ancient Egyptians that these decorations were balanced on each side. A carving would often have two columns of hieroglyphs. One column was to be read from left to right. The other was to be read from right to left. The figures in the text showed how it should be read. For example, if the signs faced left, such as 🦅 or ✋, they should be read from left to right.

Hieroglyphs are written in blocks. The ancient Egyptians loved things to be **symmetrical** and pleasing to the eye. For example, a string of signs would ideally be grouped in a block-like formation. The signs spell the name of the Sun god, Ra. When grouped, they look like this: . The taller pictures are balanced with wider pictures.

symmetry perfect balance along a centre line

Something's missing

You may notice that there is no punctuation or spacing between the hieroglyphs. There are also no vowels. Scholars still don't know today which vowels were used. This means that nobody knows exactly how to pronounce any of the words in hieroglyphs.

Chapter 2

A hieroglyphic history

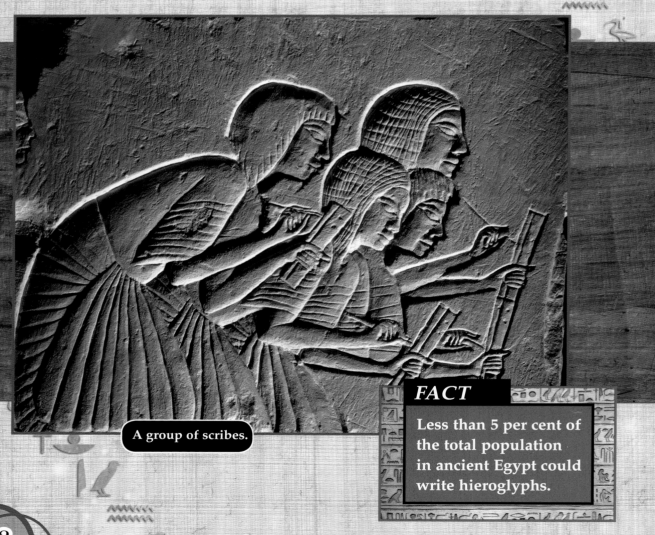

A group of scribes.

FACT

Less than 5 per cent of the total population in ancient Egypt could write hieroglyphs.

The ancient Egyptians developed hieroglyphic writing in around 3200 BC. Originally, there were between 700 and 800 hieroglyphs, or glyphs for short. These glyphs were used to record prayers, spells and religious texts. They were also used for recordkeeping.

By 300 BC, there were more than 6,000 signs. Only the most important people, such as the royal family, priests and government officials, knew how to write hieroglyphs. Others who were trained to read and write hieroglyphs were called scribes. These scribes copied official and legal documents that were written in hieroglyphs. A scribe went through years of training to learn the signs and how to write them. Some went to scribal schools when they were as young as 12 years old.

Being a scribe was a good job. Scribes could earn a good living. But it was not easy work. A scribe could be seen studying or working for hours on end. There was a lot to learn. A student just starting to read and write hieroglyphs needed to know the meaning of at least 200 signs. A basic knowledge of hieroglyphs was around 750 signs. A fairly skilled scribe had to know more than 3,000 glyphs.

Scribes wrote on **papyrus**. Papyrus was made from plant strips that were pounded together in a layered pattern. Sheets of papyrus could be pressed together to make a long roll. Scribes wrote with a type of brush made from reed plants. Cut reed stems were dipped in water. Then they were dipped in colours on a wooden block – like painting with watercolours. Black and red were used for most writing, while other colours were for illustration.

Papyrus

A scribe kit

papyrus writing material made from plants

Vases engraved with hieroglyphs

Craftsmen carved or painted hieroglyphs onto stone, pottery, wood, leather and metal. The first signs found on pottery or small ivory plaques, date back to 3200 BC. The earliest signs cannot be read easily. The first scribes worked with far fewer signs than later scribes. Eventually, scribes used thousands of signs.

Along with hieroglyphs, the Egyptians also used a script called hieratic. This script was like longhand. The signs were more connected and could be written faster.

Hieratic script was not carved into stone but used for common documents, such as letters. This kind of writing played an important role in the lives of everyday Egyptians.

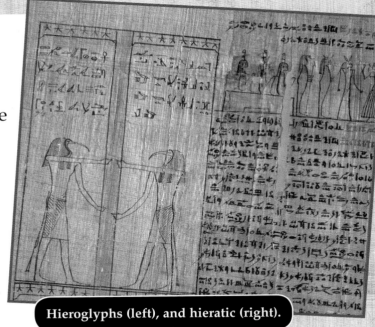

Hieroglyphs (left), and hieratic (right).

As well as being faster to write, hieratic was also always read the same way, from right to left. Special tools were used to make the script easier to write. The stems of rushes were cut to be more like a brush for this joined-up writing.

Scribes began using another script called Demotic around 660 BC. Demotic was an abbreviated script. The signs looked nothing like hieroglyphs. The letters could be written even faster than hieratic. At first, Demotic was only used for official documents and letters. It was later used for all types of texts.

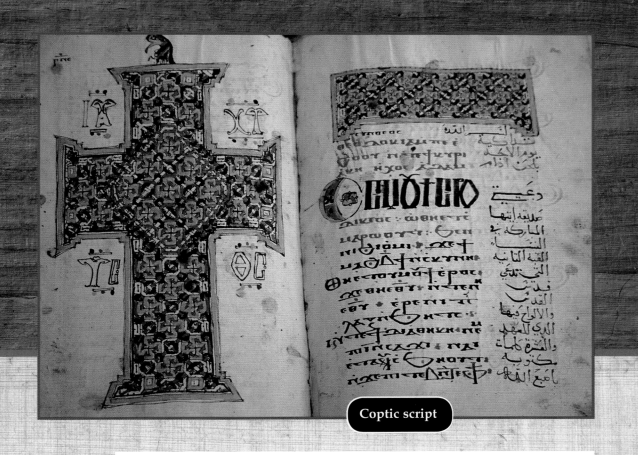

Coptic script

Coptic was the last script used to write the ancient Egyptian language. Developed around AD 200, Coptic uses Greek letters and a few Demotic signs. The name Coptic comes from the Greek word for Egyptian.

Hieroglyphs continued to be used throughout the Ptolemaic period (305 BC–30 BC). As the Romans began to rule Egypt, fewer and fewer people could read or write hieroglyphic signs. The last example of anyone writing in hieroglyphs is from AD 394. For the next 2,000 years, no one would be able to read or write the signs.

Chapter 3

Decoding hieroglyphs

The Rosetta stone found by the soldiers in 1798 was covered in hieroglyphs, Demotic and Greek writing. Copies of the writings were made and sent to scholars around the world. The Greek writing was decoded in 1802. The stone told of good deeds done by a ruler called Ptolemy V.

It would take more than 20 years to crack the rest of the code. The first scholars who looked at the stone made a mistake. They thought each sign stood for an object or an idea. The Greeks had thought the same. But none of them knew that many of the signs stood for sounds too.

Thomas Young

An English doctor was the first scholar to see that the signs stood for sounds. In 1814, Thomas Young received a copy of the stone's writing. He noticed that a sign called a **cartouche** was used to circle the names of kings and queens. He wondered if he could find the names of Greek rulers circled in cartouches. He noticed that the Greek name Ptolemy looked very similar in both Greek and Demotic. He read through the hieroglyphs and found the same result with the Demotic writing and the hieroglyphs.

cartouche oval with a ruler's name inside it

Ptolemy

The ruler's name is spelt both Ptolemy and Ptolemaios. However, his name is pronounced the same, no matter which spoken language. Young used this knowledge to match the glyphs to sounds. Young soon had a short vocabulary list of 86 words translated from Greek to Demotic.

The name Ptolemy written in both hieroglyphs (top) and Demotic (bottom).

Thomas Young's decipherment of the name Ptolemy from the Rosetta Stone text.

heiroglyph	Young's sound value	actual sound value
■	p	P
⌒	t	t
(bird glyph)	optional	o
(lion glyph)	lo or ole	l
(glyph)	ma or m	m
(two strokes)	i	i or y
(glyph)	osh or os	s

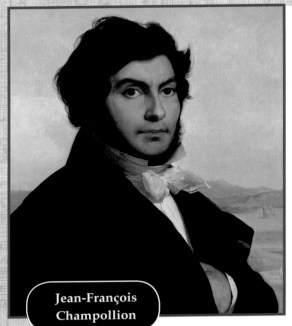

Jean-François
Champollion

Frenchman Jean-François Champollion followed Young's work closely. He took Young's vocabulary list and expanded it. After two years of work, Champollion was able to recognize the names and titles of most of the leaders mentioned in the text. He was also able to understand and explain the grammar system that was used.

At the time, many researchers believed that each hieroglyph stood for a sound. Names of rulers were written **phonetically**, just like Ptolemy's. Names such as Alexander or Cleopatra were written this way too. But in 1822, Champollion saw a cartouche that had an older, more traditional Egyptian name.

The cartouche Champollion studied in 1822.

phonetic where written symbols directly represent sounds

Champollion did not know what the first two symbols meant. But he did know that the double symbol at the end made an "s" sound. He also knew the Coptic word for Sun was "ra". He wondered if the Egyptian glyph meant the same thing. He thought the middle symbol, with its three prongs, might be an "m". Champollion also knew there had been a pharaoh called Rameses.

Names in cartouches written next to ordinary hieroglyphs.

FACT

Cartouches symbolized a loop made from a double thickness of rope. The ends of the rope were tied together. Cartouches were seen as symbols of eternity. Drawing a cartouche around someone's name made the sign into an **amulet** and protected that person.

amulet small charm believed to protect the wearer from harm

To test his idea, Champollion searched for another cartouche with the same symbols. He used this cartouche as a comparison.

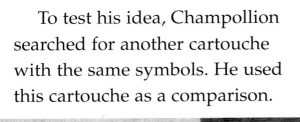

He knew the bird represented the god Thoth and used that as a starting point. By sounding out the symbols, he came up with the name of another pharaoh, Thutmose. By filling in the blanks, Champollion was able to prove that the hieroglyphs stood for both sounds and ideas.

Soon after, Champollion was finally able to read the entire Rosetta stone. He made a list of signs along with their meanings in Greek. After his death in 1832, his works were published as a dictionary and a grammar book.

FACT

The Rosetta stone was dated the same day it was carved – 196 BC, the ninth year of Ptolemy V's rule.

The Book of the Dead

Another famous text written in hieroglyphs is called the *Book of the Dead*. The *Book of the Dead* originated in the New Kingdom (1539–1292 BC). This book was a collection of spells, written on scrolls. It was also a place for scribes to record spells that would help the dead in the **afterlife**. The book was buried with the dead.

A page from the *Book of the Dead*.

afterlife life that begins when a person dies

Hieroglyphs through time

Rule of Tutankhamun

Alexander the Great enters Egypt, putting the country under Greek rule; the Greco-Roman Period begins.

Humans settle in Egypt.

Demotic is developed.

Scribes use several thousand hieroglyphic signs.

| prior to 5000 BC | 1332–1323 BC | 660 BC | 332 BC | 300 BC |
| 3200 BC | 1187–1156 BC | 305 BC | | 196 BC |

The first recorded use of hieroglyphs.

Ptolemaic dynasty (Dynasty 33) begins

Rule of Rameses III

Rosetta stone is carved.

The Greek writing on the Rosetta stone is translated.

Englishman Thomas Young translates the Demotic text of the Rosetta stone.

Cleopatra dies, beginning Roman rule in Egypt.

The last use of hieroglyphs is recorded.

30 BC	August 24, 394	1802	1814
69 BC	AD 200	August 1798	1822

Cleopatra VII is born.

The Rosetta stone is discovered.

Coptic is developed.

Frenchman Jean-François Champollion is able to read the entire Rosetta stone.

Chapter 4

Words and numbers

The hieroglyphic alphabet had 24 signs for sounds. Again, there were no signs for some vowels in English such as "u" or "o". There was also no sign for the letter "v".

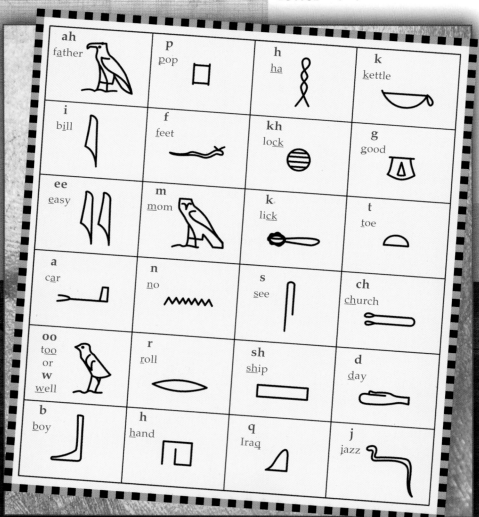

ah father	**p** pop	**h** ha	**k** kettle
i bill	**f** feet	**kh** lock	**g** good
ee easy	**m** mom	**k** lick	**t** toe
a car	**n** no	**s** see	**ch** church
oo too or **w** well	**r** roll	**sh** ship	**d** day
b boy	**h** hand	**q** Iraq	**j** jazz

Numbers in hieroglyphs were based on signs that stood for units of 10. The sign I was used to write numbers between one and nine. For example, III was three and IIII was four.

Larger numbers used more than one kind of sign added together. Tens, hundreds, thousands and other multiples of 10 had their own symbols. For example, the number 276 looked like this:

276

	1	|| 2	||| 3	|||/|| 4	|||/|| 5
|||/||| 6	||||/||| 7	||||/|||| 8	|||/|||| 9	∩ 10
100	1,000	10,000	100,000	1,000,000

Chapter 5

Write your own

Use the alphabet on page 26 to write your name in hieroglyphs. Remember that hieroglyphs were written without vowels. So, Jenny would become J N N Y. Using the letter chart, those sounds in hieroglyphs are 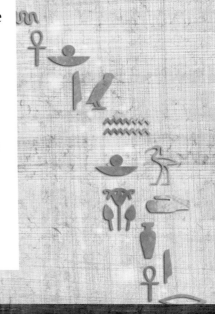. Hieroglyphs should be balanced, so this string could become . Your name may have a letter not in the alphabet on page 26. If so, it's your lucky day and you can make your own sign! And if you're feeling royal, why not add a cartouche?

How did they write it?

Cleopatra

Ptolemy

Tutankhamun

What's his name?

Pharaohs had five different names. Three names represented the gods – the Horus, Nebti and Golden Horus name. They also had a throne name and birth or family name. The pharaohs are generally known by their throne name, also called the prenomen, and their birth name, called the nomen.

The prenomen and nomen are written in cartouches. The other names are not. King Tut's names appear on the left page. The cartouche on the left is his birth name, Tutankhamun. The cartouche on the right is his throne name, Nebkheperure.

FACT

Names were important to the ancient Egyptians. They believed that if a person's name was not written anywhere, the person could not survive in the afterlife. They wrote their names in their tombs and graves in the hope that the writing would last forever.

Today, historians use hieroglyphs to learn more about ancient Egypt. Just glancing at some glyphs on a jar can tell them a lot. They can learn who owned the jar, where and when the person lived and what their beliefs were. They can learn about a ruler's rise to power and a god's special ability. Hieroglyphs tell a story, and the discovery of the Rosetta stone has made retelling the story possible.

GLOSSARY

afterlife life that begins when a person dies

amulet small charm believed to protect the wearer
    from harm

cartouche oval with a ruler's name inside it; a name-plate
    or name tag

mirage something that appears to be there but is not;
    mirages are caused by light rays bending where air
    layers of different temperatures meet

oasis place in the desert where there is water; plants and
    trees grow in oases

papyrus writing material made from plants

phonetic where written symbols directly represent sounds

symmetry perfect balance along a centre line

Ancient Egypt (History Detective Investigates), Rachel Minay (Wayland, 2014)

Ancient Egyptians (Explore!), Jane Bingham (Wayland, 2015)

Egypt: A Benjamin Blog and His Inquisitive Dog Guide (Country Guides), Anita Ganeri (Raintree, 2015)

WEBSITES

www.ancientegypt.co.uk/writing/rosetta.html
Learn all about the Rosetta Stone in ancient Egypt.

www.bbc.co.uk/history/ancient/egyptians
Discover cool facts about hieroglyphs, mummification, gods and goddesses and more.

INDEX